A GUIDE TO ACHIEVING
YOUR GOALS AND DREAMS
ONE STEP AND ONE DAY
AT A TIME

Copyright © 2017 by Lauren Daniels & Lisa King

Tiny Life Changes

All rights reserved. No part of this publication may be reproduced, distributed, or transmitted in any form or by any means, including photocopying, recording, or other electronic or mechanical methods, without the prior written permission of the publisher, except in the case of brief quotations embodied in critical reviews and certain other noncommercial uses permitted by copyright law. For permission requests, write to the publisher, addressed "Attention: Permissions Coordinator," at info@beyondpublishing.net

Quantity sales special discounts are available on quantity purchases by corporations, associations, and others. For details, contact the publisher at the address above.

Orders by U.S. trade bookstores and wholesalers. Email info@BeyondPublishing.net

The Beyond Publishing Speakers Bureau can bring authors to your live event. For more information or to book an event contact the Beyond Publishing Speakers Bureau speak@BeyondPublishing.net

The authors can be reached directly at tinylifechanges.com and at BeyondPublishing.net/TinyLifeChanges

Manufactured and printed in the United States of America distributed globally by BeyondPublishing.net

New York | Los Angeles | London | Sydney
Library of Congress Control Number: 2017955564

10 9 8 7 6 5 4 3 2 1   978-1-947256-06-4

Paperback first edition 2018
Hardback first edition 2018

ACKNOWLEDGMENTS

Our journey of writing Tiny Life Changes has proven to us the importance of change in our own lives. We realize, it is not if our lives will change, but when our lives will change. We also discovered, the most important part to change is how we react to it.

As we reflected on how we arrived at this point, it has given us a heart of gratitude. We are thankful for all of the people we have met along our journey and every experience that has shaped us into the women we are today.

Most importantly, we are grateful for the love and support of an amazing family.

We could not have accomplished what we have without our husbands Jeff and Sean by our side. Our parents, Joanne and Sal have always been our biggest fans.

As our families grow we cannot help but be so proud of our most important accomplishments, our children. We often refer to them as Team Awesome. Chad and Hillary, Kayli and Bryan, Adam and Kirsti, Sam, Grace and Dan, you truly all are our greatest gifts. Lastly, we credit HS for all of the support in writing Tiny Life Changes at lightening speed, we could not have done this without you.

Lisa and Lauren

ABOUT THE AUTHORS

Growing up, sisters Lisa King and Lauren Daniels could not have been more different. Lisa was the firstborn, an overachiever who always had her nose in a book. She knew from a young age she wanted to become a pharmacist and has enjoyed her career in this field for 30 years. Lauren, the baby of the family, was the more social of the two. She was quick to make friends and has created what she often refers to as a "village".

Lisa was living the life of her dreams with her husband and high school sweetheart, Jeff, and their three boys. With the birth of her third son, Lisa chose to hang up her white coat and stay at home with her family full time. When the U.S. economy took a downturn in 2008, Lisa's family was hit extremely hard, as were many other Americans. The real estate market crash was the catalyst for change in not only Lisa's lifestyle, but also her mindset.

Lisa had to make a choice during this time, as her oldest was off to college, and her youngest was starting preschool. She knew she had to put her white coat back on again. Working in the pharmacy was a way she could, financially contribute to her family.

As Lisa's life changed, she immersed herself in self-development. She began purchasing and reading books to lift her spirits and push through this challenging period in her life. These books could be found everywhere with Lisa. In her purse, bedside table, coffee table, bookshelves, and car.

Lisa learned that happiness and the peace and fulfillment she was seeking had to come from within. She realized that she had to change her mindset, or nothing would change. She began working on identifying negative thought patterns and word choices that she was using throughout her day. This is when she came up with the mantra "turn it around". These three simple words were a reminder to keep only the thoughts that made her stronger.

Over the past ten years, through tiny changes in her thinking, Lisa has created a shift in her life and has achieved the fulfillment she was seeking. She is passionate about empowering others to achieve their health and wellness goals. As a health and wellness advocate, she shares tips both inside and outside the pharmacy. She supports many clients in her community on their road to becoming healthy and happy. Lisa is a true believer that, by making necessary changes, one can create the life they have imagined.

From a very young age, Lauren always had a strong feeling that there was something she was meant to do. Unlike Lisa, Lauren found her calling a little later in life.

Lauren married her husband, Sean, right after college graduation. The two were very active volunteering in their community while raising their two older children and just had their third child. Lauren was enjoying her growing family and could never have anticipated that her life would soon take a very sudden turn of events.

After her third pregnancy, Lauren went for a routine mammogram, because of her family history of breast cancer. With one phone call, her life went from a time of joy to something unimaginable. "I'm sorry to inform you that the results of your biopsy tested positive for breast cancer."

Lauren was a 35-year-old mother of three and was facing cancer surgery. She was now preparing for a bilateral mastectomy, reconstruction surgery, and a full hysterectomy. At the time of her diagnosis, her three children ranged in age from one to eleven years old.

After Lauren's surgery, the baby she had waited for for seven long years, she could no longer lift or even hold. The exhaustion and pain she experienced made it impossible for her to even walk to the ball field to see her son play baseball.

During this extremely trying time, Lauren learned that she had to make a conscious choice to push through her pain. She began to realize that a positive mindset was her best choice to get her through her recovery. This was not always easy, and the theory of taking one day at a time quite literally had to be broken down to taking one hour at a time.

As Lauren became stronger, she felt incredibly fortunate for all the support from her husband, parents, sister, and her village. She realized cancer is never welcome at any age, but being a mom with cancer comes with a whole different set of obstacles. Through small shifts in her thinking, Lauren went from a "why me" attitude to a feeling of gratitude. She learned that making tiny life changes in her thought process was simply the only way to tackle life's biggest challenges.

Lauren founded the Happily Ever After League (HEAL) in 2004, just six months after her breast cancer diagnosis. She then opened the HEALing House in 2007, to support mothers and their families through cancer recovery. Lauren began to realize it was her cancer diagnosis that brought her to her life's work. Lauren is also a certified life coach and works with clients to live life to the fullest, even during a difficult time and to become the best version of themselves.

Lisa and Lauren have learned that, in life, even an adverse situation can bring about positive change, and they both live their lives by this example. Sharing what they have learned through their own life challenges is their gift to you.

The life of your dreams is one tiny change away.

PREFACE

Tiny Life Changes is an interactive guide that includes the inspiration, tools, and affirmations needed to point you in the direction of your goals and dreams.

> **MOVING FORWARD** is moving forward. Each step in the right direction will get you closer to your goal.
> - Lisa King

You can rewrite your story. Visualize the ending, and implement tiny life changes that are needed to move forward. Just take the next best step, and you will be on your way to the life you have imagined. Every day, we get the chance to change, so, instead of saying "one day", say "day one".

The time is now!

START TODAY, a tiny change is better than no change at all.

-Lauren Daniels

What Tiny Life Change can you make today to bring the desired outcomes you want tomorrow?

What are you waiting for?

TINY Life changes

**LAUREN DANIELS
LISA KING**

A GUIDE TO ACHIEVING
YOUR GOALS AND DREAMS
ONE STEP AND ONE DAY
AT A TIME

No matter how big the task, goal, or dream, all you must do is make a **COMMITMENT** to change. This is the first step in the right direction, and you will be on your way with one **TINY CHANGE** at a time.

—Lauren Daniels

What are you committing to? Do not just try in life. You are either in, or you are out. Give it your best effort, and get going.

Instead of saying,
"Today I will try to _____,"
say, "Today I will make a tiny change to
_____."

What are you committing to change?

The secret of getting **AHEAD** is getting **STARTED.**

Sally Berger

Setting a goal is important and necessary. Goal-setting can be overwhelming, but, if you break goals down into smaller steps, they will become more attainable.

You cannot expect to see a change, unless you make one. A change, even a tiny one, will bring you one step closer to your goal.

STEPS TO YOUR GOAL:

1. Make a decision.
2. Put your goal on paper.
3. Tell someone your goal.
4. Plan your first steps.
5. Take one step at a time.
6. Segment your goal into small steps.
7. Celebrate your small successes.
8. Work through your fears and setbacks.
9. Give yourself permission for a redo, and keep moving forward.

What goal will you set for yourself?

Keep only the thoughts that make you **STRONGER.**

Author Unknown

Tiny changes in your word choice will create the positivity needed to get you where you want to be. Turn your thinking around, and make a better choice.

START BY MAKING TINY REPLACEMENTS:

Replace fear with courage.

Replace doubt with trust.

Replace hopelessness with hopefulness.

Replace sadness with joy.

Replace anxiety with peacefulness.

Replace being unappreciative with being grateful.

When Lisa went back to being a working mom again, she had to turn around her word choice. She changed from thinking, "I am so tired," to, "I am grateful that I have the ability to contribute to my family." This word choice pushed her through her day, as opposed to making her feeling stuck.

What words will you replace today?

I will replace _____

_____

_____

with _____

_____

_____

You'll never change your life until you change something you do daily. The **SECRET OF YOUR SUCCESS** is found in your **DAILY ROUTINE.**

John C. Maxwell

The Best Things in Life are Free~

Make some Tiny Life Changes that cost nothing and can turn your health and thinking around.

- Go for a walk.
- Take deep breaths.
- Get fresh air.
- Go out in the sunshine.
- Get some rest.
- Have a cup of tea.
- Meditate.
- Take a bath.
- Read a book.
- Volunteer.
- Write in a gratitude journal.

What tiny change can you implement into your daily routine to improve your mood?

DESTROY NEGATIVE THOUGHTS when they first appear. This is when they're the **WEAKEST.**

— Songide Makwa

Each day, you have a choice: you can choose a good attitude, or you can choose a bad one. The day will go 100 percent better if you choose a good one.

> When you cannot change a certain situation, the best thing to change is a certain someone. **YOURSELF!**
>
> *Lauren Daniels*

- Change your mind.
- Change your behavior.
- Change your perspective.
- Change your communication.
- Change your environment.
- Change the company you keep.
- Change your outlook.

As a survivor, Lauren had to work on changing her thoughts of going from living in fear of cancer to trusting that everything was going to be okay.

What tiny life change will give you a more positive life?

Put your **HEART, MIND,** and **SOUL** into even your smallest acts. This is the **SECRET TO SUCCESS.**

Swami Sivananda

Success can be yours just by making some Tiny Life Changes to turn your thinking around.

MOVE FROM	TO
Criticizing	Being accountable
Putting others down	Lifting others up
Having no plan	Setting goals
Gossiping about people	Talking about ideas
Feeling entitled	Feeling thankful
Thinking negatively	Thinking positively
Working alone	Collaborating with others

What Tiny Life Changes can you make to achieve the success you are striving for?

CREATE what you want, as opposed to staying stuck where you do not want to be.

Lauren Daniels

It is up to you!

WHERE YOU ARE	WHERE YOU WANT TO BE
Disinterested	Energized
Upset	Inspired
Discouraged	Fulfilled
Frustrated	Valued
Bitter	Grateful
Uninterested	Passionate
Stuck	Engaged

Is there something keeping you from where you want to be?

What is one thing that will make you want to jump out of bed in the morning?

REST and **SELF-CARE** are so important. When you take time to replenish your spirit, it allows you to serve others from the overflow.

— *Eleanor Brown*

TAKING CARE OF YOURSELF first allows for change to manifest in your life. You also send yourself a message that **YOU ARE WORTH TAKING CARE OF** when you make healthy choices.

Lisa King

What tiny changes can you commit to today that will lead to better health?

- Drink more water.
- Work more steps and walking into your day.
- Stock your fridge with healthy foods.
- Avoid toxic chemicals in your environment.
- Choose colorful fruits and vegetables.
- Take a break.

What will you do to take care of you?

Wherever you are, BE ALL THERE.

Jim Elliot

MINDFULNESS
Being present without judgement
In every moment

MINDFULNESS TOOLS

- Meditate
- Breathe deeply
- Listen to music
- Observe your thoughts
- Spend five minutes doing nothing
- Spend time doing what you love most
- Spend time with loved ones
- Devote time to being still
- Call an old friend
- Unplug from technology
- Smile

Foster seeds in your mind that transform your thoughts. Make a conscious choice to turn your thinking around and come from a place of acceptance, love, compassion, and joy.

What tiny change can you make to be present in every moment?

Don't believe everything you **THINK.**

Allan Lokos

Make the following Tiny Life Changes in how you frame your thoughts to bring positive change to your life.

REPLACE:

I can't with I can.

I won't with I will.

I shouldn't with I should.

I couldn't with I could.

I am unable with I am able.

Lauren had many doubts when starting the Happily Ever After League (HEAL). She had to go from a can't do to a can-do attitude, and, now, thousands of individuals have been served from a change in her mindset.

What words can you use to reframe your thoughts and turn your thinking around?

You will either step forward into **GROWTH**, or you will step backward into **SAFETY**.

Abraham Maslow

How will you answer the 5 W's to make Tiny Life Changes and move forward?

Who do you want to become?
_____
_____

What is your next best step?
_____

When can you commit to making a Tiny Life Change?
_____

Where do you see yourself one year from today?
_____
_____

Why not start now?
_____
_____

CHOICE, not circumstances, determines your **SUCCESS.**

Author Unknown

Each day is another opportunity to make positive changes. The attitude you start the day with will ultimately determine the outcome of your day.

Positive Attitude

=

POSITIVE OUTCOME

I CHOOSE TO BE

**forgiving
peaceful
patient
kind
grateful
happy
thankful
joyful
content
caring
hopeful
inspiring**

When Lisa headed back to the pharmacy, she chose to make it a goal to bring a smile to her elderly patients. She knew the quickest way to bring a smile to herself was to give one away. This became a bright light for Lisa, and left her with a grateful heart at the end of the day.

What will you choose?

In order to **LOVE** yourself, you must **BEHAVE** in ways that you **ADMIRE**.

Irving Yalom

What are qualities you would like to be known for? Choose the ones that you would like to work on, and add them in your daily routine one by one. They cost nothing, but can increase your value and bring great success.

Be enthusiastic.
Be passionate.
Be on time.
Be prepared.
Be positive.
Be coachable.
Be a risk-taker.
Be accountable.
Be flexible.

Be curious.
Be creative.
Be engaged.
Be laser-focused.
Be confident.
Be a good listener
Be self-reliant.

Which one of these will you work on first?

Accept **RESPONSIBILITY** for your life. Know that it is **YOU** who will get you where you want to go, **NO ONE ELSE.**

Les Brown

What I can take responsibility for when making Tiny Life Changes?

My thoughts
My words
My actions

What will you work on next?

Thoughts _____

Words _____

Actions _____

CHANGE your THOUGHTS and you can CHANGE your WORLD.

Norman Vincent Peale

Positive affirmations reframe your thoughts and keep you on track to achieve your goals and dreams.

Positive affirmations are very powerful and can bring positive changes in behavior.

- Set aside some quiet time daily for positive affirmations.
- Choose a goal.
- Choose affirmations you believe to be true.
- Repeat the affirmations silently or aloud and envision yourself reaching your goal.

Affirmations

TO USE NOW, THEN ADD YOUR OWN!

I am becoming the best version of me.

I am confident that I have the ability to achieve my goals.

I will venture outside of my comfort zone.

I will only keep the thoughts that make me stronger.

I will see the greatness within myself.

I will live the life I have imagined.

I will change for the better.

I will make tiny changes daily, until I reach my goal.

I can make positive change in my past habits and patterns.

I will take care of myself and acknowledge my own self-worth.

I will give myself permission for a redo.

I will become who I am meant to be.

My own affirmations:

GOALS

Start today, and write your goal on paper.

Dr. Gail Matthews, a psychology professor at the Dominican University in California did a study that showed if you write something down, you are 42 percent more likely to make it happen.

Write down the goal you are working on:

_____
_____
_____
_____
_____
_____

Write down who you will share your goal with:

_____

_____

What will be your first step(s)?

_____

_____

_____

_____

Write down your challenges or fears and what you learned from them. How did you redirect yourself and stay committed to your goal?

_____

_____

_____

_____

_____

So is this one day or day one?

There is no better time than now to make the tiny changes needed to live the life of your dreams.

Notes

Notes

Notes

www.ingramcontent.com/pod-product-compliance
Ingram Content Group UK Ltd.
Pitfield, Milton Keynes, MK11 3LW, UK
UKHW020244240426

12048UKWH00026B/1599

9 781947 256064